YoungWriters
— Est. 1991 —

Lest We Forget

Echoes Of Conflict

Edited By Lynsey Evans

First published in Great Britain in 2024 by:

YoungWriters®
Est. 1991

Young Writers
Remus House
Coltsfoot Drive
Peterborough
PE2 9BF
Telephone: 01733 890066
Website: www.youngwriters.co.uk

All Rights Reserved
Book Design by Ashley Janson
© Copyright Contributors 2023
Softback ISBN 978-1-83565-182-7

Printed and bound in the UK by BookPrintingUK
Website: www.bookprintinguk.com
YB0579S

Foreword

Our latest poetry competition, *Lest We Forget*, focuses on war and the impact it has had throughout the years. We asked young poets to pen their thoughts on the subject, either reflecting on the horrors of war, the impact on those left behind, or a hope for resolution. With conflict still rife in the world today, it's a subject that cannot and should not be avoided. It's important to acknowledge the sacrifices, fear and pain that some people still have to face, and these young poets have done just that.

Some of the poetry in this collection focuses on the direct experiences of war: the sights, sounds, smells and emotions, creating a vivid picture in the mind's eye. Other poets explore the difficulties faced by those who are left behind, and the emotions of waiting for your loved ones to return, uncertain if they ever will.

Here at Young Writers our aim is to encourage creativity in children and to inspire a love of the written word, so it's great to get such an amazing response. The result is a collection of thoughtful and moving poems in a variety of poetic styles that also showcase their creativity and writing ability. Seeing their work in print will encourage them to keep writing as they grow and become our poets of tomorrow.

I'd like to congratulate all the young poets in this anthology. However they chose to express their thoughts and feelings, the resounding effect is a powerful one: a continuous battle for freedom, hope, and above all, a cry for peace.

Contents

Airlie Primary School, Airlie

Lyra Bain (9)	1
Kayla McNeill (10)	2
Jamie Robertson (10)	3
Zoe Anne Robertson (8)	4
Evie Hefer (10)	5
Sorsha Constable (8)	6

Aldborough Primary School, Ilford

Salaar Khan (10)	7
Maryam Khonat (11)	8
Baiza Jabeen (10)	9

Belton CE Primary School, Belton

Annabelle Hammond (11)	10
Katy S (10)	11
Harriet Hatton (10)	12
Toby Walker (10)	13
Rebekah Overton (10)	14
Anaya (10)	15
Michael Pollard (11)	16
Leyland (10)	17
Gabe (10)	18
Charlie Light (9)	19
Ivy Emerson (10)	20
Lacey (9)	21
Libby (10)	22
Olivia Edström (11)	23
Ethan Smithers (10)	24
Pandora (9)	25
Jessica P (10)	26
Daisy Rees (10)	27
Liam (10)	28
Maddy (11)	29
Brooklyn Callaghan (10)	30
Fred Thorpe (9)	31
Vivek K (10)	32
Saxon (10)	33
Alesha (11)	34

Dairy Meadow Primary School, Southall

Inaya Ahmed (8)	35
Ishika Ramesh (8)	36
Rakshitha Jegatheesh (8)	37
Ishika-k Kaur (9)	38
Ameera Sab (8)	39
Neriah Marfo (8)	40
Belina Hamde (8)	41
Aarav Garha (9)	42
Riya Patel	43
Aahena Arora (8)	44
Ayana Fakhar (8)	45
Makiyah Carriman (8)	46
Husaina Abid Rajabali (8)	47
Rayyan Dlashi (7)	48
Aayan Sadiq (7)	49
Moustafa Mehez (8)	50
Aroush Chaudhry (8)	51
Aayush Chahar (8)	52
Asmaa Mohamed (9)	53
Rayyan Sheikh Bue (8)	54
Gunreet Arora (8)	55
Saron Abeye (9)	56
Sahib Sidhu (8)	57
Sharvi Gandhi (7)	58
Nimrat Kaur (7)	59

Discovery Primary Academy, Walton

Ethan Clark (11)	60
Kaya Hilliam (10)	61
Alexis Wright (10)	62
Patrick Ion (10)	63
Enoch Migiro (10)	64
Benjamin Baisden (10)	66
Hattie Bruce (10)	67
Ananya Sahoo (10)	68
Lola Lawson (11)	69
Olivia Cotton (10)	70
Rosie Mckie (10)	71
Ebony Holcombe (10)	72
Gracie-Mae Franklin (10)	73
Ehsan Noori (10)	74
Corey Osbourne (10)	75
Dora Jovanov (10)	76
Brogan Stepenson (10)	77
Lukas (10)	78
Scarlett Onwonga (10)	79
Amelia Osprey (10)	80
Crystal Bailey (11)	81
Evie Terry (10)	82
Anna Luiza Martins (11)	83
Konnor Marshall (10)	84
Frank Zawistowski (10)	85
Eduarda Rebuzzi (11)	86
Kai Parsons (10)	87
Amelia Smith (10)	88
Thomas Starkey (11)	89
Violet Winter (10)	90
Demi-Rose Baxter (10)	91
Aminah Aamir (11)	92
Damijanas Luksas (10)	93
Basem Awadallah (10)	94
Amelia Dauksaite (10)	95
Amelia-Lilly Atkinson (11)	96
Alexia Sulaj (10)	97
Kristians Liepkalns (10)	98
Hassan Shabbir (11)	99
John-Junior Smith (10)	100
Una Haughton-Poroga (11)	101
Matthew Dickinson (10)	102
Farah Asadi (10)	103
Summer Smith (10)	104
Martynas Zymantas (10)	105
Noemi Sousa (11)	106
Adegunna Esther (10)	107
Tomas Middleton (10)	108
Isaac Oliver (10)	109
Red Dair (10)	110
Alex Goode (10)	111
Jessica White (10)	112
Saeed Asadi (10)	113
Gwen Tanner (10)	114
Daniel Weightman (10)	115
Amber Berridge (10)	116
Daniele Buzaite (10)	117
Ava Taylor (10)	118
Lexi Land (10)	119
Gavriils Drinks (10)	120
Hollie Goode	121
Jayden Goodrum (10)	122

Haileybury School, Hertford

Cameron Logan (13)	123
Anita Akande (13)	124

Hope Academy, Newton-Le-Willows

Jacob Worsley (13)	128
Riley Williams (11)	129
Ruben Wahab (11)	130
Elliot Hankin (11)	131
Rowan Watkinson-Boyle (11)	132
Emily Horn (11)	133
Elliot Birley (11)	134
Lily O'Garra (12)	135

Percy Main Primary School, Percy Main

Ellie Herbertson	136
Daisie Luckley	138

Charlie Kiely	140
Lucas O'Donnell	142
Layla Redpath	144
Noah Ewaskow	146
Alesha Blacklock	148
Macy-Leigh Huntley	150
Sierra Taylor	152
Cory McDonald	154
Thomas Chirnside	156
Lucas Baker	158
Carter Jones	159
Luke Lye	160

Platanos College, Lambeth

Tahseen Haque (13)	161

Rockmount Primary School, Upper Norwood

Delia Thomas	163
Arthur Campagna (9)	164
Anouk Mirza (9)	165
Joni Pople (10)	166
Zofia Hervais-Adelman Sęk (10)	167
Maggie Hayes (10)	168
Ava	169
Nerys Thomas	170
Michael Poulmah (9)	171
James Jack (9)	172
Adanna Jornet-Umunnakwe (10)	173
Emmanuel Chikwendu (5)	174
Samuel Tuke (5)	175
Lola Jackson (5)	176

St Mary's School, Gerrards Cross

Minnie Cotterell (9)	177
Daya Khinda (9)	178
Jaya Bass (10)	181
Jayna Master (8)	182
Sienna Bika (9)	183

Tabor Academy, Braintree

Kawsar Ahmadi (12)	184
Aaliyah Aminu (11)	186
AJ Cooper (13)	187
Oloruntobiloba Olubiyi (15)	188
Mia Madison Sanguineti (11)	189

The Poems

Remember The People

R emember the people who fought in the Great War.
E ven if they're gone we remember the great sacrifice.
M y great, great grandfather fought in the Great War too.
E very day we think of them even if they're gone.
M any people are still fighting in war.
B ecause they made this sacrifice, we now have a better world.
E ver loved and now we lay in Flanders fields.
R emember on the eleventh day of November we start our silence.

Lyra Bain (9)
Airlie Primary School, Airlie

Remembrance

R ight by each of our sides.
E ach one and other.
M ust always remember.
E ach scared and injured soldier who sadly left us.
M ornings and dark, frightening nights fighting for us.
B y our sides.
R emember the nail-biting war.
A nd all the frightened families.
N eeding love and support.
C hildren who lost loved ones.
E ach one of us remember.

Kayla McNeill (10)
Airlie Primary School, Airlie

Remember

R emember the brave bold soldiers.
E motions flooded families' hearts.
M others mourned the news of sons lost in brutal battles.
E veryone evacuated their homes to stay safe.
M uddy, bloody trenches made soldiers miserable, wet boots and trench foot.
B ig bombs blew up buildings bellowing.
E veryone wears poppies to remember fallen soldiers.
R emember to wear a poppy.

Jamie Robertson (10)
Airlie Primary School, Airlie

Remember

R emember, remember, the eleventh of November.
E veryone has tears flooding down.
M ercy for people who have lost loved ones.
E veryone has two minutes' silence at 11 o'clock.
M en had to fight in war and families had to evacuate.
B eware, bombs are coming.
E ven though they may be gone they will still be inside your heart.
R est in peace.

Zoe Anne Robertson (8)
Airlie Primary School, Airlie

Bravery

B efore the war we had peaceful times.
R emember what we gave.
A lways be grateful for the life. You have our sacrifices which were made to save.
V alour was our last gift.
E very life lost. Now a memory.
R emember what we gave.
Y our world is now yours to live in. Free from tyranny.

Evie Hefer (10)
Airlie Primary School, Airlie

Remember

R emember the dead and alive.
E lderlies lost hope.
M emorials built to remind us of war.
E ntire towns destroyed.
M y life and yours were bought.
B eware, war is coming.
E motions are sad and lost.
R espect the people that are still fighting.

Sorsha Constable (8)
Airlie Primary School, Airlie

Women At War

There's a girl who drives the train,
There's a girl who sweeps in the rain.
A time she'll never forget,
The time she was full of fret.
Wondering how they'll finish,
Crashing buildings, one second demolish.
Picking up metal trash,
From the tank crash.
People die in front of her,
On top of their heads there are bullets that shower.
Children full of curiosity,
When their parents die, they run around with ferocity.
On the 11th day of November, after 11 hours,
On the battlefields grew flowers.

Salaar Khan (10)
Aldborough Primary School, Ilford

War Girls

There's this girl who saves lives,
And the girl who scrambles for good,
The girl who shouts in pain,
While food is fed.
Strong, outstanding and fit,
Runs with a candle lit,
No longer in pain,
We scramble in vain.
Never missing a life,
Operations go slice.

Farming without regret,
We reflect.
Instead of rummaging in bins,
We serve in tins.
Strength, grip and sticks,
We pay homeless in sobs of happiness,
Without forgetting with no regret.

Maryam Khonat (11)
Aldborough Primary School, Ilford

War Girls

There's a girl covered in blood from head to toe,
She is treating someone who fought against his foe,
And covered in sweat
That's a job she won't regret.

Even though she is tired,
She tries not to get fired,
And tries her best,
Until that she won't rest.

On the eleventh day, the eleventh month and the eleventh hour,
On battlefields grew flowers,
She has her hands full of equipment,
For people she won't forget.

Baiza Jabeen (10)
Aldborough Primary School, Ilford

In Flanders Fields

I see badly wounded soldiers,
I see a bomb exploding in the distance.
In Flanders fields,
I hear the sound of men shouting,
I hear the sound of guns shooting. *Bang!*
In Flanders fields,
I taste the smoke from the bombs deep in my throat,
I taste the dirt landing in my mouth,
In Flanders fields,
I smell the rotting flesh of fallen men,
I smell wet mud in the trench,
In Flanders fields,
I can touch the cold metal on my gun,
I can touch the only poppy growing,
In Flanders fields.

Annabelle Hammond (11)
Belton CE Primary School, Belton

Life In The Trenches

I could smell mud dripping down the walls.
Smoke rising as they fall;
I could feel the grit on my feet.
The wire scratched my hands as I reached.
I could hear the soldiers groan in pain,
As my happiness started to drain.
You could hear the boom of the guns in the air;
It gave the soldiers quite a scare.
There was a lot of death;
The reason for the rotting flesh
I could smell on the soldiers.
I wiped the mud off my shoulder.
I hope I can come home soon.

Katy S (10)
Belton CE Primary School, Belton

Life In Flanders Fields

I see the deep, dark muddy
Trenches - nothing growing except a
Single poppy in a mud bath.

I hear the soldiers shouting
And a gunshot - a sharp one.

I smell the rotting flesh
Of the fallen comrades.

I taste the iron from the blood
Along with the bombs and gas.

I feel the mud-filled trenches
And the cold metal of the guns.

In Flanders fields, lest we forget.

Harriet Hatton (10)
Belton CE Primary School, Belton

Terror Of The Trenches

I hear the bangs of gunshots, spraying across the field.
I see the poppies red as blood, the last symbol of hope.
I smell the rotting flesh of my fallen comrades.
I taste gas filling the trenches with its toxic stench.
I feel the heavy metal of my gun as I take down an enemy.
Many go out though few shall come back.

Toby Walker (10)
Belton CE Primary School, Belton

Bodies And Guns

I can see bloodstained poppies and hurt soldiers.
I can hear guns loading, soldiers screaming and rats squeaking.
I can smell the smoke of the bombs and rotting bodies.
I can taste the smoke from the gun that I'm holding.
I can feel the wet, brown mud beneath me and my heavy, rusty gun that I am holding.

Rebekah Overton (10)
Belton CE Primary School, Belton

The Day We Fell

I see lifeless soldiers scattered across fields of poppies,
I hear loud bangs of gunshots ending my comrades' lives,
I taste smoke and mud on my lips,
I smell dead bodies and rotting flesh,
I feel the cold beneath my feet and the metal gun within my hands.
In the bright red poppy fields.

Anaya (10)
Belton CE Primary School, Belton

Tears In The Trenches

I see my comrades dropping like flies.
I hear the bangs of frag grenades and the popping of gunshots.
I smell the immense fear of all my dying friends.
I taste blood as I have been shot in the chest.
I feel splintering wood from my rifle gun barrel.
Soon, I will be dead.

Michael Pollard (11)
Belton CE Primary School, Belton

Life In A Trench

I see blood-red poppies swaying in the breeze.
I hear the boom of grenades exploding in the enemy trench.
I taste nothing but smoke in the air.
I smell the gas of the bombs that exploded nearby.
I touch my fallen comrade who has been hit.
Lots go out, few come safe.

Leyland (10)
Belton CE Primary School, Belton

There Is No Hope

I see the brown, damp mud
Dancing in front of my eyes.
I hear gunshots ringing in my ears.
I can smell the stench of gas.
I can taste the blood of my fallen comrades.
I can feel the cold, wet water,
Slowly rotting away my feet;
I won't last long here.

Gabe (10)
Belton CE Primary School, Belton

The Old Trench

I see my fallen friends and the blood-red poppies.
I hear the guns banging and planes soaring.
I smell the toxic gases wafting through the trench.
I taste the brown sludge that is supposed to be food.
I feel the cold metal of my gun.
Down in the deep, dark trench.

Charlie Light (9)
Belton CE Primary School, Belton

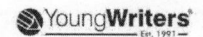

Life In The Trenches

I see the ruby-red poppies blowing,
I hear the gunshots go pew, pew as they whistle past my ear,
I smell chemicals exploding as a gust of smoke goes flying by,
I taste the mud,
I taste the gas,
I touch my fallen comrade lying in the mud,
In Flanders fields.

Ivy Emerson (10)
Belton CE Primary School, Belton

Life In The Trenches

I see blood, the colour of bright red poppies,
Dancing in the deep, dark mud.
I hear guns splattering towards my enemies.
I smell smoke, ashes, and fear.
I taste nothing but dirt, poppies and air.
I touch poppies, mud, him and blood.
In Flanders fields.

Lacey (9)
Belton CE Primary School, Belton

Terrible Trenches

I see the lonely poppies grow
I hear the vicious guns blow - *bang, bang, bang*
I smell the rotten flesh of my fallen comrade
I taste nothing but dirt and smoke
I feel stones on my knees as I crawl
Toward a nearby shot
In Flanders fields.

Libby (10)
Belton CE Primary School, Belton

Remembrance

I see the exhausted soldiers fighting for their lives,
I hear the bleeding gunshots echo over the field,
I taste the fear of my fellow comrades,
I smell the stench of the trenches,
I touch the paper-thin poppies grow through the mud.
As we remember.

Olivia Edström (11)
Belton CE Primary School, Belton

Life In The War

I see red, beautiful poppies and the angry people.
I hear gunshots and explosions. *Bang!*
I smell dirty comrades and sweat.
I can taste fear and soup, bad soup.
I feel falling comrades and the dirty ground.
The war isn't over.

Ethan Smithers (10)
Belton CE Primary School, Belton

Untitled

I see the luscious poppies growing in the grass
I hear grenades exploding in the air
I taste my lunch from two hours ago
I smell iron from my comrades
I feel the cold metal of my gun
We will always remember them
In Flanders fields.

Pandora (9)
Belton CE Primary School, Belton

The Day We Fell

I see the poppies, blood red,
I hear the guns that drown out what I said,
I smell the gas and the smoke,
I taste the blood, it makes me choke,
I touch my fallen comrade,
Icy cold, this must be bad.

We will remember.

Jessica P (10)
Belton CE Primary School, Belton

Remembrance Day

I see bullets flying past from soldiers
Wet mud in the trenches
Blood-red poppies thrown about in the mud
I smell a bucket of fear inside of me
I smell smoke and gas
I can touch wet mud and blood
I step on fallen comrades.

Daisy Rees (10)
Belton CE Primary School, Belton

In The Wars

I see the hard metal bullet flying past my head,
I hear the shouting of the hurt, horrible people - our enemy,
I smell fear coming from the Germans,
I taste nothing but smoke,
I touch my spade ready to dig,
In Flanders fields.

Liam (10)
Belton CE Primary School, Belton

Life In The Trenches

I see lifeless soldiers and poppies all around.
I hear loud gunshots. *Whizz! Bang!* from guns.
I taste black smoke and iron from blood.
I smell the fear of my comrades.
I touch the cold metal of my gun in Flanders fields.

Maddy (11)
Belton CE Primary School, Belton

Lest We Forget

I see poppies as red as blood
I see fallen comrades shouting for help
I taste thick smoke and fear
I smell the rotting flesh of the dead
I touch the cold skin of my fellow comrade and cry

Lest we forget!

Brooklyn Callaghan (10)
Belton CE Primary School, Belton

Life In The Trenches

I see fallen comrades lying on the floor
I hear the booming of the enemy's grenades
I taste the smoke of the cannons
I smell the rotting flesh of my enemies
I touch the cold metal of my gun
Lest we forget.

Fred Thorpe (9)
Belton CE Primary School, Belton

Life In The Trenches

I see the paper-thin poppies sink in the mud.
I hear rat ta ta from my comrade's gun.
I smell sweat from my comrade's armpit.
I taste the muddy, brown grass.
I feel the gigantic gun in my hand.

Vivek K (10)
Belton CE Primary School, Belton

Life In The Trenches

I see blood-red poppies.
I hear the fear in everyone's voice.
I taste groaning from the soldiers.
I smell smoke.
I touch the shoulder of the fallen comrade.
Lest we forget.

Saxon (10)
Belton CE Primary School, Belton

Lest We Forget

Life in a trench
I see the red poppies grow
I hear the rats scuttling
I smell rotten flesh
I taste the mud on my lips
I touch the poppies in Flanders fields.

Alesha (11)
Belton CE Primary School, Belton

The Way It Goes

Rise and shine my little luck
My favourite colour is red and black
Poppies make you remember the people who died
Poppies are no ordinary flower
Normal flowers represent nothing
But this one represents a lot of things
To show life many years ago
Remember who has passed and not
Praise the defenders a lot
They were being very selfless
The people who have died in the past
When you see them in their graves
Please make so many poppies be placed
Everybody will take this journey no matter what
I know that you're feeling down
Your relatives will cheer you up
They won't leave you behind
You know that they love you a lot!

Inaya Ahmed (8)
Dairy Meadow Primary School, Southall

Remember

R emember the people that care about us
E nd being selfish, instead be selfless
M any people died and a part of family was lost
E veryone fought for us, so let's respect them
M ost of them died for all of us
B ut those who love us fought for us
R ight before dying, they knew they'd made the right choice
A nd still today the people live in fear and wish that the war would end
N ow we realise that the soldiers died for us
C ome to buy poppies for those that have died for us
E very time on November 11th we remember the ex-soldiers.

Ishika Ramesh (8)
Dairy Meadow Primary School, Southall

Selfless Sacrifices

L ittle boys grow up to be soldiers
E nd of the day they win the war
S acrificed for our lives today
T ook a big risk only for us

W e should be grateful for sacrifices
E ast, west, north and south, guarding the country

F ought for peace
O n a big challenge to do or die
R emembrance Day is all about that
G uarding our land day and night
E arly every morning getting ready to fight
T hink about that at 11 o'clock on the 11th of November for two minutes.

Rakshitha Jegatheesh (8)
Dairy Meadow Primary School, Southall

In Flanders Fields The Poppies Blow

Between the crosses row to row,
That marks our space and in the sky,
The larks, still bravely singing fly scarce
Heard amid the guns below.

We are actually the dead. Many days ago
We lived, felt dawn, saw sunset glow
Being loved and were loved, but now we lie
In Flanders fields.

Take up our quarrel with the enemies:
To you, from failing hands, we throw
The torch; be your light to hold it upright high.
If ye break faith with us who die,
We shall not sleep at all,
Though poppies grow in Flanders fields.

Ishika-k Kaur (9)
Dairy Meadow Primary School, Southall

War And Peace!

Peace is calm and slowing,
War is terrifying and glowing,
Peace gives us the remembrance of the day,
While war breaks down Earth's peace,
Peace gives us relief and comfort,
While war gives us worries and sadness,
Peace gives us hope,
While war brings death and reminds us of soldiers,
Peace goes calmly,
While war reminds us of the Palestine and Israel war,
Peace reminds us of holidays
while war reminds us of hell
Peace is good,
War is bad.
Lest we forget.

Ameera Sab (8)
Dairy Meadow Primary School, Southall

Never Forgotten

Innocent children were endangered because their parents sadly died
Selfless soldiers saving lives but risking their own
We will never forget what they sacrificed for us
So wear your poppy and remember how they risked their lives for yours
Many soldiers in battle fell for you
You were saved by the soldiers so please
Show respect for soldiers risking their lives for you
They are gone but never forgotten
Lest we forget.

Neriah Marfo (8)
Dairy Meadow Primary School, Southall

Poppy

- **P** oppies are a symbol of remembrance.
- **O** n the 11th of November at 11 o'clock is when Remembrance Day is celebrated.
- **P** oppies raised money to help millions of sailors, soldiers, and airmen who were coming home from World War One.
- **P** oppies look different in different countries.
- **Y** ou can show peace to celebrate Remembrance Day. So take two minutes and remember those people who gave peace to our future.

Belina Hamde (8)
Dairy Meadow Primary School, Southall

The Red Field

The soldiers that fought were very brave,
They faced war in big waves,
Pigeons that helped were very smart,
They were used to send messages to those far apart.

The innocent children that died,
Spent most of their time trying to hide,
During the war there was a lot of bloodshed,
The muddy field looked like a sea of red.

A few years later, poppies grew,
Reminding us of the lives we once knew.

Aarav Garha (9)
Dairy Meadow Primary School, Southall

Poppy Day

Scarlet poppies grow on the battlefields,
And they dance like graceful ballerinas,
Among the feathery stalks,
Red poppies glow like bright little lamps,
On our warm winter coats.
They whisper, like long-lost voices,
From the forgotten fields.
I'll wear a little poppy,
As red as can be!
To show that I care for those that fought for me,
Such a delightful flower,
Oh, what a sight!

Riya Patel
Dairy Meadow Primary School, Southall

Remembrance Day

"Poppy, poppy, who are you?"
"Wear me on Remembrance Day and then you will know who I am"
"But what is Remembrance Day?"
"Remembrance Day is when you remember someone"
"But, but poppy, who are you?"
"When you wear me, everyone will know you are celebrating Remembrance Day."

Aahena Arora (8)
Dairy Meadow Primary School, Southall

Remember November

Remember, remember,
11th of November,
11th hour, 11th day, 11th month,
Two minutes of silence which is really quiet.
War had happened, please don't forget,
World War One don't forget to,
Wear a red or purple poppy.
November, November,
You are amazed at the effort
Of people and animals in the war.

Ayana Fakhar (8)
Dairy Meadow Primary School, Southall

The Army's Sacrifice

The army's sacrifice is so sad.
If I was in the army I would survive or not survive.
I wish they could all survive, but instead, some survive and some do not survive.
So sometimes it's sad for people because some people that are in their family die.
Can most people survive?
Have the people who have joined died yet?

Makiyah Carriman (8)
Dairy Meadow Primary School, Southall

Always Remember

R emember the people who died in the wars
E verybody stands in silence for two minutes
M any brave soldiers died
E ach year remember
M any people died
B rave, strong, and never gave up
E very eleventh day remember
R isking their lives for us.

Husaina Abid Rajabali (8)
Dairy Meadow Primary School, Southall

Untitled

I can see you
But you can't see me
You can feel me
But I can't feel you
I can hear you
But you can't hear me
Remember me
Remember me
Remember the member who died
In the war, for the innocent civilians
I lost my life to save yours!
So remember me.

Rayyan Dlashi (7)
Dairy Meadow Primary School, Southall

Remembrance Day

R emember your love
E veryone has a good life
M um and Dad always love you
E veryone is special
M um and Dad take you fun places!
B ad people break poppy flowers
E nter your house with joy
R emember your happy memories.

Aayan Sadiq (7)
Dairy Meadow Primary School, Southall

Untitled

In Flanders fields
Poppies blowing between the crosses
Row after row where soldiers
Risked their lives
To keep us safe
Plenty of soldiers who went to war
Never came back
Our job is to never forget them
War is a curse of God on Earth
It reminds us of hell.

Moustafa Mehez (8)
Dairy Meadow Primary School, Southall

Remember And Protect

P eople who risked their lives for us
R espect them and learn from them
O n this day we remember
T elling their stories to
E ach other, remember at 11 o'clock
C ould we improve the past and
T each this lesson to others?

Aroush Chaudhry (8)
Dairy Meadow Primary School, Southall

Remember

R emembrance Day
E very soldier was loved
M illions of soldiers died
E very year we wear a poppy
M emories of war
B ad days in war and brave battles
E very day we stand on guard for our country
R emember.

Aayush Chahar (8)
Dairy Meadow Primary School, Southall

Together

The sun has fallen, the world in rage,
We all must fix it before we lose our lives,
If we all work together, soldiers won't die,
In a blink of an eye you see the dead,
Telling you the truth, how to save us all,
Poppies growing on the fields of war.

Asmaa Mohamed (9)
Dairy Meadow Primary School, Southall

War

The First World War, the Great War
Four years of terrible war have finally ended
Life in the trenches has been cold
I am glad it's over
But I am sad because we lost so many soldiers
I hope for peace and harmony
Lest we forget.

Rayyan Sheikh Bue (8)
Dairy Meadow Primary School, Southall

War And Peace

When our army fought
We thought we would have peace
Now we have uncles and nieces
Who are in the army
We now wear a poppy
I wish that the law says
That war will be banned
And I hope
That there will be a no to war.

Gunreet Arora (8)
Dairy Meadow Primary School, Southall

Remembrance Day

Remembrance Day is about someone we have lost
It does not have to be someone we know
It can be a human or an animal
Especially horses because they had to push the guns
And the enemy is shooting at them so the good people kill them.

Saron Abeye (9)
Dairy Meadow Primary School, Southall

Untitled

- **R** emember
- **E** verybody
- **M** arching
- **E** arly
- **M** orning
- **B** ack
- **E** very day
- **R** eady to do it all again.

Sahib Sidhu (8)
Dairy Meadow Primary School, Southall

Remembrance Day

- **R** emembrance
- **E** motion
- **M** emorial
- **E** xpress
- **M** artyrs
- **B** elief
- **E** mbrace
- **R** ecollection.

Sharvi Gandhi (7)
Dairy Meadow Primary School, Southall

Remembrance Poem For Kids

- **R** emembrance Day
- **E** ncourage
- **M** emory
- **E** mpower
- **M** edal
- **B** ugle
- **E** nergy
- **R** ecall.

Nimrat Kaur (7)
Dairy Meadow Primary School, Southall

Untitled

Wrapped in our love, across the sea.
Heroes as brave as fearless lions, strong as a tiger.
Protecting what is right.
Brothers and sisters, daughters and sons.
A blanket of love, saying their last goodbyes.

Calamity and chaos in an ordinary house, drawing the silence out.
Music and mischief, a dinner with family.
A whole, big heart-warming sight, wrapped in a blanket of love.
They said their last goodnight.

Sunset walks across the sandy beaches.
Days being spent splashing in the dark, blue sea.
Enjoying the family time in the sunshine and light.
Ice cream dripping on the floor in the summer sun.
Wrapped in a blanket of love, they said their last goodnight.

Forever, to fill our memories, of our heavy hearts.
Hearing them talking, whispering, in the wind.
Their smiles radiated in the sun, with all of their might.
Always wrapped in blankets of love, they said their last goodnight.

Ethan Clark (11)
Discovery Primary Academy, Walton

Remembrance Day

Brave, bold, heroic, fearless fighters as brave as tigers,
Mothers, fathers, sons, daughters,
Protecting what is right,
But never knowing when it is going to be their last night.

Each day the thoughts wonder,
Never knowing when they're going to laugh,
Just one more time,
When they're going home to see their family,
When will it be their last goodbye?
Goodbye, goodbye.

Memories fill their head,
Their last Christmas or birthday at home,
Or their last full meal,
As they lie to go to sleep,
They can't help but hear the gunshots fire,
When will it be their last goodbye?
Goodbye, goodbye.

Sorrow will fill your heavy heart forever,
With that extra bit of grief,
Their voice will crack with tears in their eyes,
As they say goodbye, goodbye, goodbye.

Kaya Hilliam (10)
Discovery Primary Academy, Walton

For The Fallen Soldiers

Heroes, as fearless as a bear, fought on the ferocious battlefield
Brothers, sisters, sons and daughters
Having a breath, might be the last
Protect what is right, it might be the last goodnight

Not laughing with comrades and no family games
Hugs are gone
They have fallen and family is sad, find family fun one last time
Protect what is right, it might be the last goodnight

Soldiers have fallen for us
Their last turkey Christmas dinner
Their last present opening and joy and birthday whilst alive
Protect what is right, it might be the last goodnight

Memories to cherish people from war
Having voices sing sorrow, smiles come to the sun, sad in the moment
They fall again, to the end, to the end, we will remember them
Protecting what's right, it might be the last goodnight.

Alexis Wright (10)
Discovery Primary Academy, Walton

Untitled

Bloodthirsty soldiers ready for war,
They should have known what would happen before,
But when they hold hands in fear,
You might even see a little tear,
Fighting day and night,
Their body shakes from all the fright.

At home, they laugh lots with lots of joy,
And their sons playing with a little toy,
Music blasting in the air,
While the children have fun like a fair,
The stars fill up the sky,
While the adults eat pie.

Going together on a holiday,
And shouting it's the best day,
Making memories and taking pictures,
Going to the beach at night,
And feeling the beautiful delight.

Sadness now, sadness later,
They were killed by his biggest rival,
Never forget them now or later,
They fought for us against our biggest hater.

Patrick Ion (10)
Discovery Primary Academy, Walton

The Dead Lives

The fallen heroes,
Brave as an eagle,
Fought with all their might
Until their last night.
Fighting 'til their last breath,
Until what's left is death.

Enjoying with their loving loved ones,
Loving all the way,
Chuckles and smiles,
Every single day,
Fighting 'til their last breath,
Until what's left is death.

Filled with presents,
Toe to toe,
Getting clothes, drinks and games,
Getting all the fame,
Minutes turn to hours,
Guns like superhuman powers,
Fighting 'til their last breath,
Until what's left is death.

Sorrow destroys the hearts of many,
Shivers down their spines,
Cherished memories,
Every time the clock chimes.

Fighting 'til their last breath,
Until what's left is death.

Enoch Migiro (10)
Discovery Primary Academy, Walton

Field Of The Fallen

Scorching winters and roaring missiles flew through the air
Bullets glide as they fight for what's right
A huge sacrifice was made that day
All to keep evil at bay
For now today we remain safe
Let's hope it stays that way.

Warm welcomes, chuckles of joy
Cheerful voices of girls and boys
Fireplace brews and radio fills the room
Final goodbyes, a cosy atmosphere all to you
Family games, sun's rays
Now the fallen sit at their grave, once so mighty and so brave.

Christmas crackers
Daisies bloom
Fire charades and moon glooms
Night to day, day to night
Now after this, they say goodnight.

Sorrow fills the heart
Internal void of despair
Once a field of chaos now a vibrant utopia
For without them, life would be no more.

Benjamin Baisden (10)
Discovery Primary Academy, Walton

Left Behind

Remember soldiers are brave and tall,
Remember soldiers giving it their all,
Families awaited their children,
Before getting a letter,
We will remember their children,
Who died to make our lives better.

They used to have fun with their families and friends,
Perhaps dancing with huge turns and bends,
Or maybe playing football, kicking and pouting,
But later they would be crying and shouting.

Families remember armour suits,
Just as they remember big, heavy boots,
They couldn't forget the old straw hats,
Nor their last time on the back door mats.

What does the future hold for those left behind?
It holds pictures and poems filled with rhymes,
Soldiers will be remembered by all,
For standing in battle brave and tall.

Hattie Bruce (10)
Discovery Primary Academy, Walton

Memories Of Love And Kindness

Soldiers - heroic - brave as a lion,
Family and friends,
Thinking about what is right,
A blanket of love,
Now they have said their last goodnight.

Rowdy and raucous in an ordinary house,
Music and mischief,
Dinner and noise with family,
A strong warmth of love,
Now they have said their last goodnight.

A splashy sea fun time with family,
Watching the sunset shimmer and glisten,
Ice cream dripping in the warm golden sun,
A blanket of love,
Now they have said their last goodnight.

Heavy hearts with profound sadness,
Stars shine brighter than seen,
Voices whisper in the wind,
No matter what memories are filled with everyone,
Even though it's their last goodnight.

Ananya Sahoo (10)
Discovery Primary Academy, Walton

The Fallen Soldier

Brave, powerful soldiers,
As fearless as tigers,
Brothers, sisters, sons and daughters,
Fighting to protect their country,
Wrapped in blankets of love.

Last dinner at the table together,
Last time playing in the garden,
Laughs and jokes,
Last time singing songs forever,
Last time having fun together.

Last Christmas together,
Delicious Christmas dinner,
Last time giving gifts,
Making yummy treats,
The last time playing games forever,
Laughs and jokes together.
Last time pulling crackers,
Warming up near fireplaces.

Heartbroken, remember all the good times,
Quiet houses, filled with sadness,
Seeing their smiles no more,
Not like the good times anymore.

Lola Lawson (11)
Discovery Primary Academy, Walton

The Fallen Soldiers

The soldiers are saviours,
They are as brave as bears,
But the confident soldiers,
Have now fallen into a deep, dark hole.

That day would be their last,
Their last dinner,
The last time laughing with their comrades,
Their last time with their family,
That day would be their last.

That night would be their last,
Their last time going to a friend's or family's house,
For birthdays, Easter or Christmas,
Playing with their families and,
Saying goodbye for the last time,
That day would be their last.

Hearts filled with sorrow,
The people fled where they fought,
We will remember them day and night,
No matter what,
We will remember them.

Olivia Cotton (10)
Discovery Primary Academy, Walton

Remembrance Day

Strong, fearless soldiers,
Brothers, sisters, cousins and daughters,
Fighting for the country and for its rights,
Making it their very last night.

The very last meal,
Very last laugh and play at home,
Never know when you will ever get a hug again,
Making it feel like the worst last night.

Last ever holiday at the beach,
Last time seeing chocolate eggs at Easter,
Last ever Christmas meal,
Very last birthday at home.

Making it the best last night,
The family left with all the memories,
They're feeling very sorrowful,
When hearing their voices from up above,
Making their hearts smash into a million pieces,
Making it their very last night.

Rosie Mckie (10)
Discovery Primary Academy, Walton

The Fallen

The more the paint washes away,
The more the flowers grow,
Sisters, brothers, sons, daughters, dads and mums look we won,
Heroes, gods, soldiers you may be gone,
But at least we won,
Fearless soldiers fight for the right.

They laughed, they played, they won the game,
Yet they can't go back again,
It was complete, now it's defeat,
Happiness and chaos,
This is the way to obey us.

Christmas dinner is full of cheer,
Trick or treat, who got the treat?
Season to season, spring to summer,
Or did I stutter?
Leaving on your birthday is a little scream.

After you went we wished you had come,
We drowned our sorrow,
In you being our soldier.

Ebony Holcombe (10)
Discovery Primary Academy, Walton

Remember The Lost

They rise at dawn,
To fight for our lives,
Risking their own,
Just to see ours thrive.

Immortal spheres,
Forever in our head,
Spend no more time with close ones,
But instead, lay with the dead.

No more chaos and clatter,
Filling their homes with glee,
No more friendly fun,
On holiday with their family.

No more chit-chat,
With their close ones and friends,
No more noisy nights with loved ones,
Our hearts are heavy when it all comes to an end.

A profound sorrow, forever in our souls,
We eternally mourn their endless sleep,
No matter the time, day, or month,
We will remember them,
Timelessly buried deep.

Gracie-Mae Franklin (10)
Discovery Primary Academy, Walton

The Fallen Heroes

The brave soldiers who were fearless and fought for our freedom,
Young men and women,
Bravely fighting in the conflict,
For their family and friends,
Before falling,
And taking their last breath.

The house was filled with chaos and clattering,
Music blasting from the radio,
Pillow fights,
Camping out in the dark starry nights.

Carving pumpkins,
Hanging out on the beautiful beach in the sunny summer,
Blowing out candles,
And shoving their face in colourful cakes.

Hearts filled with profound grief,
Memories to comfort you,
Hearing their laughing and seeing their warm smiles,
Their voice whispering in the howling wind.

Ehsan Noori (10)
Discovery Primary Academy, Walton

The Poppy Floor

So ideas of war for our country,
And now they may rest in peace,
They were amazing to us,
And we wouldn't have our country without them.

Soldiers and family members die and are lost,
People hope the soldiers survive,
Poppies everywhere,
Only plant around there,
After the war, everything was defeated except for them.

Soldiers now are probably in a better place,
It is sad though there is doom and danger everywhere,
You can barely hide from it.

We sleep better than they did so be grateful,
The war is over,
Soon we sleep to everything,
We will see them when grieving,
Rest in peace.

Corey Osbourne (10)
Discovery Primary Academy, Walton

Remembrance Day

Soldiers as brave as a tiger, as heroic as a bull,
Protecting their land, fighting for what is right,
Unable to see the future,
On and on they fight in fright.

Never forgetting the last goodbye,
The fortnight before the fight,
Last laugh with their comrades, last time at home,
So on and on they fight in fright.

Never forgetting the last celebration,
The last birthday, Christmas, Easter,
The blinking lights and the dazzling decorations,
On and on they fight in fright.

Our hearts are filled with sorrow,
Revere memories,
Missed by all,
On and on, they are remembered.

Dora Jovanov (10)
Discovery Primary Academy, Walton

The Remembrance

Soldiers are the opposite of incompetent.
Confident heroes, quite a sight.
Fighting day or night.
Fighting for what's right.

Normal houses, nothing special.
Yet everyone is happy with what they have.
Playing games together.
The last word to come a week away.

The week after was Halloween.
Only a few days.
Dressing up in scary costumes, hyper and ecstatic.
Before they say their last goodnight.

Families are forever heartbroken.
Celebrating the lost lives of many.
Happy for what they did for their country.
Still mourning the loss of the moral people.

Brogan Stepenson (10)
Discovery Primary Academy, Walton

Remember

The hero who died for us,
And got dragged away from their home,
To a dead field,
At day and night,
They watch their friends fall down,
They think, will this be my last goodnight?

The brave children,
Wives, mums, dads,
Learn the news of the bloodthirsty soldiers dying,
They cry about their lost ones,
And thought it was unfair how they got killed.

The people crying about the lost ones,
And never seeing the men, or women again.

The people will cry about the lost ones,
Then later they will get over it,
And start new lives and not be sad anymore.

Lukas (10)
Discovery Primary Academy, Walton

Remembrance

Remembering all heroic soldiers,
Who have fallen for our country,
Brothers and sisters, fighting for their life,
Doing what's right,
Families couldn't say goodbye.

Having lunch with your family,
Wouldn't know it was your last destiny,
Hearing people chattering,
Children giggling and laughing.

Dancing with the sea,
Hearing people scream,
Seeing all the sand,
But remembering all the blood going through my hand.

The broken hearts and sadness,
I think it's my time,
Seeing many poppies grow,
Looking at my own grow.

Scarlett Onwonga (10)
Discovery Primary Academy, Walton

The Fallen Soldiers

Brave soldiers, fighting to protect everyone,
Grandparents, uncles, sons and daughters,
Trying their best,
Spreading kindness and love.

A house full of happiness and joy,
Having music on the radio, singing out loud,
Lots of noise and now quiet as a mouse,
The last meal in the warmth.

Splashing like a dolphin in the sea,
Seeing children making sandcastles with joy,
Spending time at the beach,
Long sunset walks.

Hearing them say their last words,
The wind whooshing over and over again,
Tearing us with heavy hearts,
Hearts filled with sorrow.

Amelia Osprey (10)
Discovery Primary Academy, Walton

The Soldiers That Have Fallen

Brave, fearless like kangaroos
Dad, mum, sister, brother, husband, wife
Rushing there, got to protect
In the morning we will remember them

In one happy family, they were,
Funny, mischievous, having the best time
A best friend to everyone they met
In the morning we will remember them

Noisy as a cat meowing
Sun, ice cream, fun time with family
Holiday fun in the pool
Playful as a meerkat

Filled hearts of sadness
The sun putting joy back into them
They're whispers from heaven
They will be remembered as the sun goes down.

Crystal Bailey (11)
Discovery Primary Academy, Walton

Elated Rest To Eternal Rest

To remember our past and our fallen kin.
Soldiers hoping to hear the family din.
Grass will die and poppies bloom.
Singing soldiers meet their doom.

Elated nights and solemn days.
Putting their life at stake.
Eternal blossoms and smiling faces become hurt.
Many are dazed.

When a lust for care and keep and just
Becomes the one who paints the evening.
Makes us weep and feel like grieving.

We sleep so well and are at our best.
As for the soldiers eternal rest.
Their kin, weeping in sorrow.
Will soon smile, seeking the morrow.

Evie Terry (10)
Discovery Primary Academy, Walton

The Fallen Ones

They are as brave as dragons
Fearless as lions, they are the fallen ones
Wrapped in blankets across the sea
They are the bravest of the bravest

They shall not feel the warmth
They shall see the love
We will never forget because we will always remember
Poppies will come
Poppies will go
But the fallen ones will never escape

Sorry and grief across the sea
They have fallen
But they fell with love in their hearts
They have fallen for us so we have to be thankful
They fought for all of us
So we have to fight for all of them.

Anna Luiza Martins (11)
Discovery Primary Academy, Walton

The Fallen Soldiers

The soldiers who fought for our country,
Thank you for keeping us safe,
You are all fearless like lions.

Their families will always remember them,
They will remember the time they spent together,
And all the holidays they had.

As a child they played, had fun and created memories,
They helped people at home if they needed help,
They will not be forgotten.

They will not be forgotten,
They will be wrapped in a blanket of love
And now they say goodnight.

They march beyond the sky of love, beyond
We make no more pain.

Konnor Marshall (10)
Discovery Primary Academy, Walton

The Brave

Fearless warriors, wrapped in a dove.
They were as pure as a dove.
No longer will they feel the wind,
Because they died for their kin.

No longer will they chatter,
And join in with all the clatter.
No longer will they thrive,
Because they have died.

No more family fun,
As they got their duties done.
No more activities in the sun,
Because they got their duties done.

Their souls radiated by the sun,
As they got their duties done.
Their souls flow through the wind,
They'll be remembered by their kin.

Frank Zawistowski (10)
Discovery Primary Academy, Walton

Os Bravos Soldados Poderosos

Ferocious, powerful, fearless as a lion
Brothers, sisters, sons and daughters
Fighting to protect our country
Wrapped in a blanket of love

Last dinner together
Laughing, talking altogether
The noisy house is now as quiet as a mouse
Enjoying playing music

Putting up the Christmas tree, giving gifts, putting up decorations
Playing at Christmas as a family
Having dinner together
And this is the day they said their last goodnight

Heartbroken
Remembering their smile
Good memories
Heart filled with sorrow.

Eduarda Rebuzzi (11)
Discovery Primary Academy, Walton

The Fallen Soldiers

Brave, powerful, fighting
Until their last breath,
Uncles, dads, sons,
Lost in war
Even the poor.

Once an ordinary family,
Music and playing,
The house is never quiet,
Eating at the table,
Laughing with comrades,
Nobody is angry.

Happy families laughing,
Taking photos, playing with kids,
Always warm, never dull,
Nobody will pull.

Sadness throughout,
Who knew the photo would be their last?
Remembering their voices,
And no more noises,
We will always remember them.

Kai Parsons (10)
Discovery Primary Academy, Walton

Memories

Braver than lions,
Left to roam England's foam,
Forever march with glory,
We say goodbye.

Calamity chaos in an ordinary house,
Familiar faces and family fun,
Smiles and laughter - a heart-warming sight,
Sleep together, goodnight.

Splashes of laughter in the Cerulean Sea,
Peaceful walks on the sandy beach,
A friendly family's fun in the sun,
Shine upon our tears goodbye.

Fearless warriors,
Forever march with glory,
Go off to battle, singing with hope,
We miss you, goodnight.

Amelia Smith (10)
Discovery Primary Academy, Walton

For The Soldiers That Have Fallen

Sleeping on the ferocious battlefield,
Shooting the guns they wield,
Fearless as bears, they march,
Fathers, mothers, sisters and brothers.

Eating with fellow comrades for one more time,
Hugs for one more time,
Family games for one more time,
Family fun for one more time.

Gingerbread men being crunched at Christmas,
Turkey being munched at lunch,
Christmas trees sparkling,
Opening presents one more time.

People mourn,
Solemn from the wars,
As the days pass,
We will remember them.

Thomas Starkey (11)
Discovery Primary Academy, Walton

The Fallen Ones

They fight like horses,
They're fearless like lions,
They wrap in joy,
But once he was a little boy,
Until they went to war,
Then grief was a shield,
Their sorrow would grow.

We wait in the two-minute silence,
We think about who we lost,
Remember them with poppies,
The cameras are on now,
It is as quiet as a mouse.

We will remember them, everyone,
They're not here,
They're in our minds,
When the sun comes up,
We will remember this,
My last goodnight,
My love.

Violet Winter (10)
Discovery Primary Academy, Walton

Heavy Hearts Into Holes In Your Heart

Being happy on the beach,
Into watching over the sea,
Fearless warriors and brave lions,
Celebrations to funerals and bones.

Calamity and chaos,
Smiles into tears and tears into your drink,
Laughter into darkness,
And rowdiness to loneliness.

Ice cream dripping onto the sandy, wet beach,
Talking to your friends,
To the voices in your head,
And the wind went there all the time.

Poppies and butterflies to darkness and dead flies,
Your family being there to never there,
When it is time to fight.

Demi-Rose Baxter (10)
Discovery Primary Academy, Walton

For The Ones Who Sacrificed

As brave as a tiger, as fearless as a lion.
Parents, siblings, sons and daughters.
Protecting us bravely.
As they curl up in a blanket of love they have their last goodnight.

No more music, no more giggles, no more silly and fun
No more cuddles and time with family.

Sunset walks on the beach, dripping ice cream,
Sand in shoes on holidays as they say their last goodnight.

Forever in our heavy hearts, their whispers through the wind,
Their smiles in the sun, they are forever wrapped in a blanket of love.

Aminah Aamir (11)
Discovery Primary Academy, Walton

Sacrifices

A day in our life,
Remembering the people who died,
The fearless soldiers,
Fighting all day and night,
Sons and daughters
Couldn't even say goodbye.

Sitting by the beach,
Listening to the sea,
Having ice cream, hearing seagulls scream,
A journey home, seeing poppies grow.

Grandparents and parents having a good time,
Children wouldn't know it was their last time,
Courageous crusades marching upon us,
Booming and running,
Blood baths in front of us.

Despair within poppies,
Having to see all the bodies,
Waiting for sunrise,
With poppies by my side.

Damijanas Luksas (10)
Discovery Primary Academy, Walton

The Immortals

Soldiers, as brave as a fearless bear,
Trying to protect us,
And trying to care.

Chattering, clapping, and having some chaos,
Sitting with their family eating their dinner,
Always profound in their inner.

Sharing amazing,
Great love,
As happily as a,
Pure white dove.

They will still carry on,
Living in our minds,
All of the memories,
Come in all shapes and kinds.

All of us,
Will be mourning,
No matter the time,
Evening or morning.

Basem Awadallah (10)
Discovery Primary Academy, Walton

The Immortals

Fearless warriors fighting for their lives,
As brave as lions, trying to protect us.
Brothers and sisters have fallen away...

Ordinary things happening,
Loud noise, music playing, TV playing
On and on, non-stop.
People walking around the house,
Tables full of people, ready for dinner.

Holidays at the beach,
Splashing and diving.
Spending time with family and friends,
Shivering in the coldness
While the waves are whooshing.

Sadness spreading across,
One by one.
Memories to cherish.
Smiles fading away.
Forever, we will remember.

Amelia Dauksaite (10)
Discovery Primary Academy, Walton

Wounded Warriors

Remembering brave soldiers,
Boldly fighting in battle,
For all their people in the light,
To say their last goodnight.

Houses full of love and warmth,
Full of kindness and care,
Fun in the sun with family,
Soon to turn into despair.

Warriors fighting for their peace,
People dying, screaming and crying,
Fear drowning them alive,
Hopeless families petrified
For their loved ones.

Always remembered by their families,
Hearts filled with sadness,
Innocent people sacrificed,
Remember them till dusk.

Amelia-Lilly Atkinson (11)
Discovery Primary Academy, Walton

Our Fallen Fighters

Remembering the courageous crusaders,
They sacrificed themselves across the sea,
Conflict formed all around,
Defending us for our safety.

A pleasant family,
Chattering filled the home,
Family never separating,
Now they feel alone.

Eating together at the table,
No seats to spare,
But now the tables are empty,
Everyone's in despair.

They shall be cherished,
From dawn to dusk,
As fearless fighters,
And fantastic family men.

Alexia Sulaj (10)
Discovery Primary Academy, Walton

Wounded Soldiers

Heroes fearless as lions,
Brothers, sisters and mums,
Saving what was right,
Wrapped in blankets of kindness
And they had their chance
Of saying goodnight.

Courageous crusaders,
Bloodthirsty warriors,
Battling for victory,
Battle till dawn tonight,
Wounded by pain and blood.

Unfair for all the heroes that died,
Tables not full of joy,
Homes not full at all,
The field is in despair.

Memories of all the soldiers
Who have fallen,
You can hear their voices
In the fields,
Poppies growing,
All that's left is sadness.

Kristians Liepkalns (10)
Discovery Primary Academy, Walton

The Fallen Soldiers

Heroes, brave as a fearless dragon,
As fast as a cheetah, smarter than a parrot protecting what is right,
Fight what is wrong.

Ordinary things, the house filled with noise, guns, fighter jets,
Brave soldiers risking their lives to save us, fight what is wrong.

Holiday by the beach, playing in the sea,
Waves covering the sand, soldiers marching on the grass.

Heart filled with sadness, memories falling out,
People resting, people falling, resting in heaven.

Hassan Shabbir (11)
Discovery Primary Academy, Walton

Wounded Soldiers

Remembering the soldiers who have fallen in battle to England's foe,
Saying their last goodnight,
Blood-covered blankets,
Wounds covered in blood,
Courageous crusaders,
Heroes are as fearless as a lion.

They went to battle with songs,
They were young,
Steady and aglow,
With their faces to the foe,
The field is a despair.

As they're wishing,
Dynamite, they go up with their foe,
There is a kind spirit hidden from sight.

John-Junior Smith (10)
Discovery Primary Academy, Walton

Sacrifice

Bloodthirsty soldiers,
Fighting in battle,
Families worried,
Thinking the enemies are a hassle.

Houses filled with happiness, smiles and laughter,
Jokes and chatter,
TV and music,
Dancing all around.

Holidays abroad,
Ice cream and hot dogs too,
Hey! Excuse you,
You just stole my shoe.

No longer with us,
Hearts filled with sorrow,
Hear their voices,
Think of them now,
Think of them tomorrow.

Una Haughton-Poroga (11)
Discovery Primary Academy, Walton

The Brave Soldiers

Fallen, brave, as fearless as dragons
Brothers, cousins, sons and sisters
Fearless soldiers fighting to protect our country

The house is filled with mischief
No room left on the table
Rooms filled with the warmth of a family

Holiday at the beach
Making sandcastles, playing beach ball
Sunset walks, playing in the sea

Heart filled with sorrow
Memories to cherish, seeing their smile
Remembering good times.

Matthew Dickinson (10)
Discovery Primary Academy, Walton

Remembrance

Remembering our warriors,
The country's saviors got saved
By our remembering fighters,
Their faces were bladed.

Chatting and having fun,
Music blaring at the party,
People dancing and singing,
Grabbing iced tea.

The field is covered with bodies,
Screaming and shooting with bombing,
Surrounded with bloody bodies,
People throwing bombs and bombarding.

Hearts filled with despair,
I couldn't even stare,
Broken hearts and sadness,
Only enter if you dare.

Farah Asadi (10)
Discovery Primary Academy, Walton

Remember

A captain who must lead people,
A captain who needs them to sacrifice their lives,
Soldiers who listen to commands,
Soldiers who are ready to fight,

Behind the barriers of the battlefield,
Waiting for a siren to begin,
Protecting their captain,
Protecting their country.

Rising sun,
Falling moon,
Time to say goodbye,
To the soldiers who die in darkness.

We will remember them.

Summer Smith (10)
Discovery Primary Academy, Walton

Our Fallen Soldiers

Remembering the soldiers who saved our lives.
They have skill,
They are fearless,
They are unbeatable.

Soldiers were with their families eating before the war.
Preparing to be brave.
In war trying to save our country.

When the war was over, many soldiers died.
But they saved our country.
After the war, the poppies grew in the same place.
We buy poppies to show respect and to remember them.

Martynas Zymantas (10)
Discovery Primary Academy, Walton

Remember

I remember the determined soldiers,
With black empty souls, fighting for us,
They shall never grow old.

They were brave and fearless as lions,
Brave as courageous crusaders,
Brave fighters, bloodthirsty soldiers,
Battle day in and day out.

They fought until they were dead,
They thought they were going to combat until victory,
But instead, they fell on top of their enemies.

Noemi Sousa (11)
Discovery Primary Academy, Walton

Remembrance

Mingling with their friends
Eating with their families
Noise and chatter from houses
We shall always remember them

Holidays at the beach
Playing by the sea
Smiles and laughter
Buying ice cream

It shall turn to lightness
And not to darkness
We shall hear faded voices

Heart-filled sadness
As we buy poppies
We shall keep remembering them.

Adegunna Esther (10)
Discovery Primary Academy, Walton

Remembrance Day

The soldiers were powerful men,
They were brave, brave soldiers,
The soldiers were fearless,
Fighting for what is right.

Poppies to remember them,
Sadness throughout the house,
It is now quiet as a mouse,
They will never return home.

We will never forget them,
We will always feel grief,
Full of sorrow in our minds,
For all of the time.

Tomas Middleton (10)
Discovery Primary Academy, Walton

Remembrance

Brave, strong heroes -
Fearless and bold
Brothers, sisters, sons, and daughters
Mothers, fathers, and families
Fighting for their lives
Sadly passed away

Family and friends saying
Their last goodbyes
And having their last meal

Fun holidays, sitting by a warm fire
Last Christmas and last family reunion

Cherishing memories,
Depression of lost loved ones,
Hearing their voices,
Seeing their smiles.

Isaac Oliver (10)
Discovery Primary Academy, Walton

Remember Those Who Have Fallen

Fallen, fearless, brave as tigers,
Going to take their last step through the door,
Having to break the law for the war,
We will remember those who have fallen.

Family fun will end,
When it's time to go to bed,
Enjoy it, it might be your last goodnight,
While protecting those who have fallen,
We will remember those who have fallen.

Red Dair (10)
Discovery Primary Academy, Walton

The Fallen

Fearless soldiers fight for the right,
So, they can say their last goodnight,
Fighting on the battlefield,
Protecting their lives,

Blood washes away,
Flowers begin to grow,
Sisters and brothers,
Mothers and fathers,
Look we won,

Remembering them,
Every year,
Wearing poppies,
Thinking of them.

Alex Goode (10)
Discovery Primary Academy, Walton

The Fallen Soldiers

Fearless warriors, brave as lions
Protecting our land,
Now they have said their last goodbye.

Noise and nonsense in an ordinary house,
Cavity and chaos drowning out the silence,
Dinners with the whole family,
Now they have said their last goodnight.

Sunset walks,
Bathing in the hot sun,
Watching TV with family,
Now they have said their last goodnights.

Jessica White (10)
Discovery Primary Academy, Walton

Missed Soldiers

Brave as lions
Dead soldiers protect us
And our country
Fought for their lives
To save our future.

Sad families, have to remember
Killed family members in their minds
They cry and remember the memories
They had together.

Sad for their loss, family members
Stay depressed and miss
The time they had together
Sad families cry
When they think about it.

Saeed Asadi (10)
Discovery Primary Academy, Walton

Fallen, Fearless Fighters

Fallen, fearless fighters.
What did they see?
When they fought for freedom,
Across the foamy sea.

Left to forget the ordinary things:
The clatter of plates,
The buzzing of rowdy radios.
The warmth of the raging fireplace.

Left to forget the sights
They will now never see.
The sun flying across the moonlit Earth,
The blow of the warm breeze.

Gwen Tanner (10)
Discovery Primary Academy, Walton

Remembrance

Soldiers marching into battle
Buildings scattered everywhere
Fighting for the people in need
Protecting the country.

Not nice, not good
People fight
Brothers and sisters
Countries and countries
Both are the same.

Loved ones, friends and family
Have been lost in a war
Because of the people
Who started it all.

Daniel Weightman (10)
Discovery Primary Academy, Walton

Poppy Day

Brave and proud soldiers,
We remember them every year,
Sadness and sorrow felt by everyone,
We remember them on Poppy Day,

For the fallen soldiers,
We have two minutes' silence to remember,
We wear poppies every year,
We remember them on Poppy Day.

Amber Berridge (10)
Discovery Primary Academy, Walton

Remember

Brave soldiers,
Fight day,
After day,
And night,
After night.

Poor sister,
Poor mother,
Poor father,
Crying inside,
Will see you tonight.

Servicemen are there,
Fighting in blood,
Warriors alive,
The heroes,
The soldiers are skilled.

If you want,
I will go,
Through the pictures
Tonight.

Daniele Buzaite (10)
Discovery Primary Academy, Walton

Remembrance

No more giving presents
No more gathering around the tree
They don't hear the festive music
Just so their families could be free

A mother mourns for her children
She cherishes the memories
We will all remember them
Forever wearing our poppies.

Ava Taylor (10)
Discovery Primary Academy, Walton

Remembrance Day

Brave soldiers fighting,
Tall soldiers protecting,
The soldiers fought for us,
Making their family proud,

Remembrance Sunday every year,
Poppies worn to remember them,
Silence to remember them,
We will remember them.

Lexi Land (10)
Discovery Primary Academy, Walton

Remember

All day, all night
The soldiers will fight
The battle is fierce
But the heroes
Shall stand tonight.

We remember the soldiers
As fierce as lions
But they can't grow old.

They are muscular and brave
But they are still fighting
In a pool of blood.

Gavriils Drinks (10)
Discovery Primary Academy, Walton

Remembrance

I know you will,
Go through pictures,
Tonight,
That is,
Always alright.

Memories to fill our hearts,
I'll remember your smile,
Forever and ever,
Wrapped in blankets of love,
Now they have said
Their last goodnight,
Full of love.

Hollie Goode
Discovery Primary Academy, Walton

Poppies

Brave and courageous soldiers,
Holding their guns,
Serious faces,
Getting ready to fight,

Now, we remember them,
Wearing poppies,
Making poppies,
We will remember them.

Jayden Goodrum (10)
Discovery Primary Academy, Walton

War

A lone dove, high in the sky,
Soaring above the battlefields.
Down below came a soldier's anguished cry,
His fate was sealed.

The dove continued on and the screams faded away,
The dove was headed for the city.
In a waste, the streets did lay,
The sight wasn't pretty.
Bodies lying in the streets,
Smelling of rotting meats.

Past the city, the dove flew,
Towards the coast.
The sea was a deep blue
And the battle was at its utmost.
Soldiers fought on the beaches,
Ships fought in the sea.

Meanwhile, back home,
Soldiers are marching into war,
Cheered by admiring crowds
Not knowing that ahead, there was only death and gore.
Up ahead formed dark clouds
A sign of things to come...

Cameron Logan (13)
Haileybury School, Hertford

Letters

I watched you march off into the distance
With the band banging their drums and hundreds of other naive boys marching with you
I cheered you on, I helped pack your bags
Such a mistake, such regret
As the bodies come back over the weeks
You'd be lucky to have a complete body come back, if it came back

Instead you would just get a letter
But I don't ever want to see you again
If it means you are still alive, so stay alive
You never write to me, I see my neighbours receiving letters from their children
Where are yours? When will you send one?

I get a letter saying you are a corporal now
And that you're doing well in the war
So where are your letters?
No word has come from you, it's been months now
And no letters, not one

I got a letter
The sergeant in charge of your division
Sends his apologies for my loss

I got another letter
Saying that they are having difficulty transporting his body and belongings

Lest We Forget - Echoes Of Conflict

One more letter
Saying that I must be prepared because the body is not in one piece
The next day, a coffin is on my doorstep
I went back inside, if I ignore it, it won't be true

I left the coffin out there for three days
I did not leave my house
I did not look at it even when it rained
At last I went outside, I had to see if it was true

He was in the coffin
His arm lying next to his shoulder
His leg was separated from his body
And his foot was missing

Was this the boy I raised?
Almost unrecognisable with all his scars
Covering his pale skin
Was this the man I watched leaving?

On his chest was a pile of letters
All the letters he never sent
All the letters I waited for
I never imagined I'd get them this way

I read the one on the top of the pile
He apologises for not being strong enough to send me these letters
For having doubts about being in the war

For wanting to quit
If he disappointed me

He thought I was disappointed

My neighbours try to comfort me
But their pats of pity on my shoulder
Make me feel worse for how could they understand
Their warm comfort
Just reminds me how cold my son is

People pass by offering condolences
And someone has the audacity to tell me
That I should not cry, I should be proud
My son died for our country

I should be proud?

My son came back to me as a cold, broken corpse
And I should be proud

My son is dead, while yours is holding your hand
As you tell me to be proud
Proud that I will never hear my son's voice again
Proud that I will never see his beaming eyes again
Proud that I will never feel the warmth of his hugs again
I should hold back my tears because he died for a country
A piece of land that we just happened to live on

He died in a war that is still ongoing
People are still fighting and suffering
While my world has stopped
The reason I'm still here has left

I read one of his letters each day
He told me everything about what he did
He wrote so many letters and I read them all
I finished reading the same day that the war ended
I wrote a letter to him and put it on his grave
I write a new letter each year on Armistice

I will write him letters 'til the day I die.

Anita Akande (13)
Haileybury School, Hertford

The Mark They Left

R emember the hope that they felt
E xplain the loss that was left behind
M emorise the pain from the loss
E veryone should be remembered
M ean what you say on the day of remembrance
B reathe peacefully knowing you're safe because of their sacrifice
E xcel in your everyday life for they could not
R eady to remember them in the future to stand together

This is the sad reality of war.

Jacob Worsley (13)
Hope Academy, Newton-Le-Willows

Untitled

"This war is terrible," they said.
"I miss my family," they said.
They are scared and they are nervous.
You might be thinking, who are these people?
Well, these are called refugees.
They want their families back.
And their home and pets back.
So instead of violence use kindness
And then all wars will end.

Riley Williams (11)
Hope Academy, Newton-Le-Willows

Lest We Forget

To my fallen protectors,
War is a terrible place,
For the people who weren't the age for it,
Many lives lost,
In return, we show our respect,
Christmas is a good time,
When all the war was put aside,
A great time and a relief for the soldiers,
But many lives were lost and the war was still won.

Ruben Wahab (11)
Hope Academy, Newton-Le-Willows

The Sacrifices They Made

The sacrifices they made,
For people to be free,
The sacrifices they made,
So they don't have to flee.

Some had to fight,
Others had to flee,
But in the darkness there's light,
That saved you and me.

The sacrifices they made,
They were big and they were true,
But don't worry, soldiers,
We won't forget about you.

Elliot Hankin (11)
Hope Academy, Newton-Le-Willows

The Lost

All of the loss in the war
Then the tears that had to pour
Everyone who had to fight
Even though it was not right

The worst things have happened here
It has been going on for more than a year
Coming now from present day
Everything is good today

We shall remember the lost
Who died for our cost.

Rowan Watkinson-Boyle (11)
Hope Academy, Newton-Le-Willows

The Lost Souls

We remember the lost ones,
Who gave their souls,
Who lifted up,
Who set their goals.

We remember the lost ones,
Who gave their souls,
Who stood by our enemies for all their people,
Who died,
I wish you a great time in heaven.

Emily Horn (11)
Hope Academy, Newton-Le-Willows

Untitled

All those men who died
They may rest in peace
At least they will forget
All those awful memories

All the disaster and flames
Gave many people the last chance
To say someone's name
All those grenades and toxic gases
Made many family members
See loved ones pass.

Elliot Birley (11)
Hope Academy, Newton-Le-Willows

Remember, Remember The 11th Of November

I wish I could go back,
Back when everything was right,
When I could fly my kite.

I wish I could make peace
When I could sleep,
And not get a peep.

Ears bleeding
From the sound of screaming.

Remembrance Day.

Lily O'Garra (12)
Hope Academy, Newton-Le-Willows

War

War looks like clustered engine shields,
War looks like jet-black bombs,
War looks like ruby-red poppies,
War looks like colossal green tanks,
War looks like rubble-like houses.

War feels like death surrounding my body,
War feels like a circle of lifeless souls,
War feels like smoke is suffocating me,
War feels like a soon-to-be obliterated world,
War feels like a prison in disguise.

War sounds like people screaming in agony,
War sounds like colossal fires flowing through the air,
War sounds like crisp rubble crunching,
War sounds like death, threatening electric towers crashing,
War sounds like wooden houses crashing to the ground.

War smells like burnt, mouldy toast,
War smells like life exiting people's bodies,
War smells like unbreathable gas,
War smells like sickly sewage entering the air,
War smells like burning animals, soon to be ash.

War tastes like ashes from the deadly fires,
War tastes like dry, flaking blood,
War tastes like gunpowder from the shot bodies,

War tastes like burnt bricks from the family homes,
War tastes like dead nature.

Ellie Herbertson
Percy Main Primary School, Percy Main

Raging War

War looks like raging soldiers,
War looks like death,
War looks like bloodstained poppies,
War looks like enormous tanks.

War feels like an uncomfortable danger zone,
War feels like the end of the world,
War feels like terrifying butterflies in your stomach,
War feels like something you will never make out alive,
War feels like being trapped in a death chamber.

War sounds like clattering bombs,
War sounds like a constant fear,
War sounds like people screaming for help,
War sounds like tumbling houses,
War sounds like horrifying echoing screams.

War smells like crackling fire,
War smells like rotten decay,
War smells like burnt rubble,
War smells like horrid burnt toast,
War smells like spicy fire.

War tastes like flaky ash,
War tastes like burnt rubble,
War tastes like soaked-up blood that will stay on you forever,

War tastes like a house full of poisonous gas,
War tastes like sickening flesh.

Daisie Luckley
Percy Main Primary School, Percy Main

War

War looks like wailing eyes,
War looks like soldiers risking their lives,
War looks like emotional people,
War looks like demolished horses burning,
War looks like hell.

War feels like enemies surrounding me,
War feels like fear,
War feels like collapsing buildings,
War feels like ravenous teachers,
War feels like the end.

War sounds like people screaming in pain,
War sounds like children saying their goodbyes,
War sounds like whizzing tanks,
War sounds like havoc,
War sounds like collapsing buildings.

War smells like cries filling the air,
War smells like burning wood,
War smells like dark smoke,
War smells like tortured bodies,
War smells like unbreathable gas.

War tastes like decrepit flaking wood,
War tastes like blood from dead bodies,
War tastes like fire filling their lungs,

War tastes like hell about to be spilt,
War tastes like rusted metal.

Charlie Kiely
Percy Main Primary School, Percy Main

War

War looks like courageous soldiers,
War looks like shaken soldiers,
War looks like gleaming guns,
War looks like destructive bombs,
War looks like torture.

War feels like fear,
War feels like a test of the highest degree,
War feels like imminent death,
Was feels like an apocalypse,
War feels like the Grim Reaper at your door.

War sounds like agonising terror,
War sounds like devastating bombs,
War sounds like buildings crumbling,
War sounds like brave soldiers risking their lives,
War sounds like surviving sirens.

War smells like thick smoke,
War smells like crackling wood,
War smells like toxic fumes,
War smells like lethal gas,
War smells like fear.

War tastes like death on the chilly breeze,
War tastes like blazing blood,

War tastes like solemn people crying about their dead relatives,
War tastes like the biggest fight of their lives.

Lucas O'Donnell
Percy Main Primary School, Percy Main

War

War looks like mighty soldiers,
War looks like fresh, beautiful poppies,
War looks like teary eyes,
War looks like camouflaged helmets,
War looks like squared bombs.

War feels like danger,
War feels like I'm suffocating,
War feels like a scratch in your head,
War feels like death threats,
War feels like endless pain.

War sounds like screeching sirens,
War sounds like screams in your ears,
War sounds like echoing cries,
War sounds like blasting bombs,
War sounds like burning fireplaces.

War smells like burning rubber,
War smells like toxic gas,
War smells like Bonfire Night,
War smells like rotten onions,
War smells like fueled engines.

War tastes like suffocating smoke,
War tastes like bloodied bodies,
War tastes like a lump in your throat,

War tastes like disgusting vomit,
War tastes like salty tears.

Layla Redpath
Percy Main Primary School, Percy Main

War

War looks like tough and brave soldiers,
War looks like a bloodstained weapon,
War looks like fear in a soldier's eyes,
War looks like blood-covered weapons,
War looks like the world is ending.

War feels like danger,
War feels like pain,
War feels like immense fear,
War feels like the apocalypse,
War feels like torture.

War sounds like deafening screams,
War sounds like yelling sirens,
War sounds like fire crackling,
War sounds like *kaboom*,
War sounds like ear-curdling bombs.

War tastes like deadly vomit,
War tastes like sickening bodies,
War tastes like blood from the dead,
War tastes like oily smoke,
War tastes like smokey fire.

War smells like Bonfire Night,
War smells like burning rubber,
War smells like crisp blood,

War smells like crackling blood,
War smells like unbreathable gas.

Noah Ewaskow
Percy Main Primary School, Percy Main

War

War looks like bloodstained uniforms
War looks like the devil's home
War looks like wrecked houses
War looks like dead people
War looks like death

War feels like death around me
War feels like an alienated prison
War feels like torture
War feels like I'm suffocating
War feels like a bad morning

War sounds like eerie gunshots
War sounds like deafening screams
War sounds like bombs blasting
War sounds like rumbling grounds
War sounds like people screaming in pain

War smells like burnt rubble
War smells like bombs creating fire
War smells like rotting bodies
War smells like fierce fires
War smells like unbreathable gas

War tastes like blood from the dead
War tastes like oily air
War tastes like gunpowder

War tastes like rotten vomit
War tastes like ashes off the burnt houses.

Alesha Blacklock
Percy Main Primary School, Percy Main

War

War looks like strong soldiers,
War looks like solemn children,
War looks like blank faces,
War looks like blood-infested poppies,
War looks like death.

War feels like hell,
War feels like bombs dropping,
War feels like death to me,
War feels like dirty mirrors,
War feels like death, everywhere.

War sounds like deafening bombs,
War sounds like screaming souls,
War sounds like families crying as their children die,
War sounds like havoc,
War sounds like shocking sirens.

War smells like burnt oil,
War smells like grey ash,
War smells like rotting bodies,
War smells like crackling fire,
War smells like death.

War tastes like ash-filled water.
War tastes like burnt rubber,
War tastes like dried-up blood,

War tastes like strong smoke,
War tastes like itching dust.

Macy-Leigh Huntley
Percy Main Primary School, Percy Main

War

War sounds like screaming soldiers,
War sounds like decaying horses,
War sounds like screeching lightning,
War sounds like dead bodies screaming.

War looks like massive tanks,
War looks like being alone,
War looks like hell,
War looks like torture,
War looks like death.

War feels like a discarded cell,
War feels like bodies around me,
War feels like I am dead,
War feels like danger,
War feels like falling.

War smells like smoggy smoke,
War smells like decrepit bodies,
War smells like fear spreading,
War smells like pepper and salt,
War smells like sadness in the air.

War tastes like blood rotting in your mouth,
War tastes like vomit oozing out your mouth,
War tastes like dirt,

War tastes like rubble,
War tastes like dead nature.

Sierra Taylor
Percy Main Primary School, Percy Main

War

War looks like carnage,
War looks like scared soldiers,
War looks like people getting shot,
War looks like terrified eyes,
War looks like destroyed buildings,
War looks like death.

War feels like soldiers dropping all around,
War feels like madness,
War feels like pain and death,
War feels like fear,
War feels like I'm suffocating.

War sounds like people screaming in pain,
War sounds like deafening sirens,
War sounds like people trekking in splodging mud,
War sounds like fire crackling,
War sounds like roofs collapsing.

War smells like Bonfire Night,
War smells like crackling fire,
War smells like rotting bodies,
War smells like burnt rubble,
War smells like unbreathable gas.

War tastes like rotten vomit,
War tastes like wispy smoke,

War tastes like burnt wood,
War tastes like deadly fire,
War tastes like drippy blood.

Cory McDonald
Percy Main Primary School, Percy Main

War

War looks like scared soldiers,
War looks like blood-covered uniforms,
War looks like rough rubbery wheels,
War looks like clogged-up gas masks,
War looks like shattered glass.

War feels like danger,
War feels like lonely land,
War feels like loud screams in your ear,
War feels like gloomy death,
War feels like you're suffocating.

War sounds like growling jets,
War sounds like deafening sirens,
War sounds like dying people,
War sounds like echoing cries,
War sounds like crackling fireworks.

War smells like burnt clothes,
War smells like rattling fires,
War smells like crestfallen death,
War smells like unbreathable gas,
War smells like deadly ash.

War tastes like smoggy air,
War tastes like sickening gas,
War tastes like dead nature,

War tastes like rotten flesh,
War tastes like mouldy engines.

Thomas Chirnside
Percy Main Primary School, Percy Main

War Looks Like...

War looks like strong soldiers,
War looks like lonely men,
War looks like destructive bombs,
War looks like smoggy skies,
War looks like death.

War feels like a danger zone,
War feels like suffocation,
War feels like death all around me,
War feels like a prison.

War sounds like screeching souls,
War sounds like bloodthirsty bombs,
War sounds like squealing sirens,
War sounds like engines roaring.

War smells like crackling fire,
War smells like unbreathable gas,
War smells like rotten bodies,
War smells like burnt rubble.

War tastes like blood from the dead,
War tastes like rotten vomit,
War tastes like oily cars,
War tastes like deadly fire,
War tastes like sickening bodies.

Lucas Baker
Percy Main Primary School, Percy Main

War

War looks like clogged air,
War looks like fearless soldiers,
War looks like strong Highland cows,
War looks like darkness.

War feels like a massive earthquake,
War feels like alienated soldiers,
War feels like broken homes,
War feels like instant death.

War sounds like deafening bombs,
War sounds like screaming children,
War sounds like crumbling houses,
War sounds like dying people.

War smells like crackling fire,
War smells like rotten flesh,
War smells like nuclear waste,
War smells like burnt rubble.

War tastes like spicy vomit,
War tastes like disgusting blood,
War tastes like oily rubber,
War tastes like ashes from what remains.

Carter Jones
Percy Main Primary School, Percy Main

War

War looks like tired men,
War looks like lonely men,
War looks like bloodshed and guns,
War looks like fifty bombs,
War looks like scared men.

War feels like the British,
War feels like unforsaken,
War feels like beams of lightning frying the ears,
War feels like bullets slicing into the side.

War sounds like deadly bombs,
War sounds like dropping houses,
War sounds like engines growling.

War smells like dreary fire,
War smells like dead soldiers,
War smells like blood and vomit.

War tastes like rotten vomit,
War tastes like people bleeding,
War tastes like scorching flesh.

Luke Lye
Percy Main Primary School, Percy Main

Be Free

From the rivers to the seas,
From the seas to the oceans,
From the oceans to the trees,
Life cannot be pleased.

The hope vanished from reality,
We love them like charity,
You want to cry when you hear the screams,
The world is much more different than it seems,
With tears rolling down your face,
It feels like home is not a place.

We want the world to be right,
But it always ends with a fight,
We want to bring hope to them,
Like a flower growing out of a stem.

Our world is full of hatred,
The smiles on their faces faded,
But we still live with hope in our hearts,
But it feels like they've been hurt by darts.

I know it's tough,
There's no place for them to laugh,
The world is a horrible place,
It seems like a disgrace.

We want it to stop,
It's like it goes on forever, non-stop,
Evilness starts to increase,
But all we want is peace,
Enough is enough, we fought for too long,
Now we must show them who's strong.

Tahseen Haque (13)
Platanos College, Lambeth

Courage

War looks like an exquisite Flanders field where resilient and hard-working soldiers lay, where picturesque and dainty poppies stay
War smells like old sickening bombs and explosive gunpowder
War sounds like bellowing screams and ear-splitting bombs and bangs from the tenacious and lion-hearted soldiers
War feels like something we could have done, something we could have saved, something that feels upsetting
It makes me feel strong but at the same time weaker
War tastes like revenge
It's jeopardising, traumatising and most of all precarious
War reminds me of these loyal and heroic soldiers who risked their lives for us
War feels like old dreams of daring soldiers
Let those dreams live on

Lest we forget.

Delia Thomas
Rockmount Primary School, Upper Norwood

Senses Of War

War looks like an endless rage of death, taking millions of hopeless lives out of this brutal word
War smells like an oblivious cloud of gas digging into the crater of a world full of desperation and terror
War sounds like a harrowing death pit of screaming, horrified, fearful soldiers
War feels like an eternal rampage of desolation
Will it ever end and let this world embrace itself into peace again?
War tastes like a mouthful of foul, burnt, disgusting rations to be eaten for months on end
War reminds me of all the selfless, sacrificial men and women who fought in deep, crammed trenches to help protect our country
Lest we forget.

Arthur Campagna (9)
Rockmount Primary School, Upper Norwood

What War Means To Me

War looks like a dark abyss of guns and dead soldiers collapsed into a carpet of corpses
War smells like smoky ashes and mustard gas with a burning, blood-curdling, rotten stench
War sounds like harsh gunfire and the deadly screams of murdered soldiers
War feels painful like a lion feasting on your neck
War creeps up on you, watching your every move until...
Bang, you're on the ground living only for a minute longer
War tastes grim, as disgusting as blood, rusty and old, putrid and bitter
War reminds me of family and friends gone, quick as a flash like how a dog snaps up its meal
Lest we forget.

Anouk Mirza (9)
Rockmount Primary School, Upper Norwood

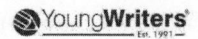

What War Truly Is

War looks like a shuddering, harrowing world filled with mortifying conflict
War smells like a field packed with gunpowder and you can sniff death everywhere
War sounds like a destructive bomb going off as soldiers boom their guns to defend them from the cold, careless souls of their enemy
War feels like a poppy of remembrance and beauty but also of bloody soldiers lying on the cold, grainy ground
War tastes of blood and furry but also of stale rations
War reminds me of all the sacrificial soldiers that lost their lives for our safety

Lest we forget.

Joni Pople (10)
Rockmount Primary School, Upper Norwood

War

War looks like sacrificial soldiers fighting relentlessly for their country
War smells like ashes and gunpowder lurking everywhere you go
War sounds like the screeching of innocent children desperately trying to get to safety
War feels like an inextinguishable fire raging across the world at the speed of an enormous roller coaster
War tastes like mouldy rations that run out in seconds
War reminds me of the Grim Reaper creeping up in my direction, seconds away from me, dead

Lest we forget!

Zofia Hervais-Adelman Sęk (10)
Rockmount Primary School, Upper Norwood

War

War looks like a violent sea of blood lapping at my heels
War smells of smoke and gas crawling through the trenches
War sounds like the screeching of soldiers just before they drop dead
War feels like being stuck in a nightmare hiding from endless raging storms which constantly tear families apart
War tastes of bitter substances which refuse to leave my mouth
War reminds me of the courageous soldiers who are willing to sacrifice their lives for their country.

Maggie Hayes (10)
Rockmount Primary School, Upper Norwood

The Sense Of War

War looks like a hazardous bomb filled with violence and conflict
War smells like ink-black smoke and pebble-grey ash
War sounds like rifles shooting repeatedly and determined soldiers shouting angrily
War feels like a filthy, freezing cold trench with dirty puddles
War tastes like mouldy bread and uncooked potatoes
War reminds me of willing, loyal soldiers and an unpleasant time we shouldn't repeat
Lest we forget.

Ava
Rockmount Primary School, Upper Norwood

Horrible War Senses

War looks like courageous, loyal soldiers fighting for their lives
War smells like fear and gunpowder shot from big, bulging black cannons
War feels like anger and jealousy invading the sky
War sounds like screaming and conflict banging and dread
War tastes like smoke and hunger and rations oh so stale
War reminds me of miracles and scarlet-red poppies but also darkness and slate-grey skies

Lest we forget!

Nerys Thomas
Rockmount Primary School, Upper Norwood

War, War, War!

War looks like a deadly, destructive nightmare
War smells like burning flames
War sounds like ghastly emotional screams as obliterating bombs explode
War feels sacrificial and heartbreaking to not see your loved ones
War tastes like bitter and pain without a new expensive ration cards
War reminds me of my special worried family who take care of me

Lest we forget!

Michael Poulmah (9)
Rockmount Primary School, Upper Norwood

War

War looks like destruction and bloodshed
War smells like burning fire and terrifying explosions
War sounds like brutal chaos and danger and disease
War feels like a terrifying nightmare everywhere
War tastes like endless oceans of filthy blood
War reminds me of devastating, chaotic violence

Lest we forget!

James Jack (9)
Rockmount Primary School, Upper Norwood

War Poem

War looks like people escaping from their homes
War smells like a cloud of deadly gas
War sounds like children crying for their fathers
War feels like the beginning of the end
War tastes like dried, scarce food
War reminds me of a world with no peace

Lest we forget!

Adanna Jornet-Umunnakwe (10)
Rockmount Primary School, Upper Norwood

Great Star

The poppies grew on the ground of the fields' floor,
The poppies grew as it was after the war,
The poppies grew and made everyone happy and grateful.

Emmanuel Chikwendu (5)
Rockmount Primary School, Upper Norwood

Lest We Forget - Echoes Of Conflict

Poppies To Remember

Poppies are special
Because they help to remember.
The suffering in wars
In the month of November.

Samuel Tuke (5)
Rockmount Primary School, Upper Norwood

War

Poppies grew when soldiers died
Poppies grew when soldiers flied
Their family cried.

Lola Jackson (5)
Rockmount Primary School, Upper Norwood

Lest We Forget

I was a free mare, frolicking through the fields.
My eyes were aglow, and my mane was rich.
Now I can hear gunshots, cries and death.
I am a war horse.
I am a fighter.

I was a peaceful horse, grunting in the stables,
My torso was muscular and my hooves were shiny.
Now, I am thin and pale, and my hooves ache.
I am a war horse.
I am a fighter.

I used to be a safe foal, protected from any threat,
Nurtured by my mother, warm in the hay.
Now, a bullet is firing my way, painful oblivion approaching.
I was a war horse.
I am at peace,
But I am still a fighter.

Minnie Cotterell (9)
St Mary's School, Gerrards Cross

Lest We Forget

As the tears fall to the ground,
And the poppies start to grow,
As we go back in time,
With the loud bangs,
And the cruel war.

The nurses are rushing,
Here and there,
Ah!
Too much shooting everywhere!
Marching through
The muddy ground
Sadness and fear everywhere.

All memories will be kept
Inside our pockets.
The soldiers march
And fight so hard
For they're
Country-loving fellows.

The soldiers were standing
Brave and tall
Ready for a terrifying adventure
That we were all gloomy about.

Lest We Forget - Echoes Of Conflict

Some became weak
And came to an end,
Some were still
To a life.

The sky became smoke
And losing friends
And teammates.
They all started to have
A broken heart
But not to give up
They carried on
For their beloved country.

Not anyone will forget
This sorrow moment.
It was 11 o'clock
And trumpets started to play.

The poppies that grew,
The soliders that flew,
Time passed,
This was called
Remembrance Day.

Might be sad
But must be remembered
And we should give thanks

To the ones that protected
Our country.

Scarlet poppies
Start to grow
They dance to the whistling birds
The sun is bright
And the sky is light blue.
Here is called Flanders fields.

This will never be forgotten
The poppy joke poem
Poppy, poppy,
Poppy, poppy, did you speak?

Wear me on Remembrance Day.
Poppy, poppy, what did you hear?
People said many soldiers in battle fell.
Oh!

Daya Khinda (9)
St Mary's School, Gerrards Cross

Lest We Forget

Lest we forget the men who fought in war,
Lest we forget the sacrifices that grew more and more,
Lest we forget the innocent children,
Lest we forget the nurses who tied wounds,
Lest we forget the nurses who died,
Lying down next to the men,
Who will never see the light of day again,
Lest we forget the tears that fell down,
While they heard the sound of war,
Lest we forget the sound of guns,
Making their ears sore,
Lest we forget someone else's point of view,
Lest we forget the few,
That lived on to tell their story,
And lived in glory,
Lest we forget.

Jaya Bass (10)
St Mary's School, Gerrards Cross

Lest We Forget

Here and there, the guns shoot by,
How I wish this was a lie,
The people who fought for our life,
Lest we forget, it'll be alright.

Life is tough, life is mean,
Those who protected us, we may never have seen,
The people who fought for our life,
Lest we forget, it'll be alright.

Scared for families, freedom and peace,
Rebuilding the country, piece by piece,
The people who fought for our life,
Lest we forget, it'll be alright.

Jayna Master (8)
St Mary's School, Gerrards Cross

Lest We Forget

The dark, gloomy night sky
And there the poppies lie
The guns shoot to and fro
Everyone kept low
We are grateful for our soldiers
Lying still like a boulder
Lest we forget the men who fought
The sadness of war, their wounds must be sore
We are thankful for the soldiers who fought for us
We must be appreciated and happy
Remembrance Day is one of the most popular days
Nor will I forget it.

Sienna Bika (9)
St Mary's School, Gerrards Cross

Whispers Of Hope

In a land where hope is sought
Afghanistan, a battle fought.
Amidst the chaos, a flicker of light,
The yearning for peace, shining bright.

Girls with dreams, hearts full of fire.
Yearning for knowledge their true desire.
But shackled by a world that denies,
Their right to learn, their wings to rise.

Yet, in their eyes, a spark remains,
A determination that never wanes.
They strive for change against the tide,
With courage and strength, side by side.

In classroom empty, their voices soar,
Whispering dreams of a future, pure.
They seek education, a path to embrace,
To break the chains, and find their place.

Let us stand with them, hand in hand,
Support their dreams, help them expand.
For in their triumph, lies a nation's grace,
A brighter future where peace finds its space.

Afghanistan, a land of resilience and might,
May peace prevail like stars in the night.

And may the girls with dreams so bold,
Find the freedom they seek as stories unfold.

In this hope, we write as one,
For a world where education has just begun.
Let us strive for peace, let us stand tall,
Together, we can make a difference for all.

Kawsar Ahmadi (12)
Tabor Academy, Braintree

Brave Poppies, Hope You Remember

P eople who risked their lives,
O ur elders who fought for us,
P laces and homes, they left,
P etals that fell so we could be here today,
I nsisting they fight as they are not to be shamed,
E nsuring that we are safe and sound,
S o let us wear a poppy and celebrate the brave and courageous men who fought until there was no strength to spare.

R emember the brave men who fought so we could be here today,
E xhibitioning their bravery and courage as they went into war,
M embers of the war, the army, are to be celebrated,
E very one of them risking their precious lives,
M others and children hoping and praying day and night that their boys and their men get home safe,
B ecause they are bringing them joy, peace and encouragement for the future,
E nsure you wear a poppy too,
R emember the men who fought for us until blood dripped and ashes smeared.

Aaliyah Aminu (11)
Tabor Academy, Braintree

I Survived...

The war rages in my blood, crying, begging, begging for more
How can I live when they die, how can I avenge those who fall?
When I look in the mirror the past stares back at me
Why did I survive? What am I meant to do?

They smile and claim, "Yes, we remember, we remember!"
But no one cares unless it's November
They gave their lives, their needs
All for your wants not your deeds

I watched them grow and I watched them go
Their spirits' poppies gone with one blow
They snuffed out their light in front of my eyes
Yet people wonder why I can't sleep at night

Everyone says, "Lest we forget"
But they're not the ones who live with this regret

They watch me squirm trying to break free
I may have survived but I've paid my fee
Here I am, trapped in these lines
Oh, how I pray, oh pray soon will be my time.

AJ Cooper (13)
Tabor Academy, Braintree

War

What good is there to say about petty rivalry?
Engaged by people of supposed 'chivalry'?
What good is in causing people anxiety?
In protecting a blood-hungry dynasty.

What good is in the tearing down of society?
What is there to protect? Notoriety?
What an irony, hiding behind the soldiers sent to die silently,
Leaving their families devastated for what?
A sick fantasy?

What good is there, endangering the lives of children who just want to live happily?
But just like the lives taken, it seems everything is done without empathy or sympathy,
War has never done anything but wreak havoc, physically and mentally,
Do we really want to bring our children up in this reality?

Oloruntobiloba Olubiyi (15)
Tabor Academy, Braintree

It Isn't Over

A cinquain

Bombers.
The end is near.
Hypnotised by Nazis
Jews being sent off. *Location?*
Run. *Flee.*

Mia Madison Sanguineti (11)
Tabor Academy, Braintree

Young Writers Information

We hope you have enjoyed reading this book – and that you will continue to in the coming years.

If you're the parent or family member of an enthusiastic poet or story writer, do visit our website www.youngwriters.co.uk/subscribe and sign up to receive news, competitions, writing challenges and tips, activities and much, much more! There's lots to keep budding writers motivated!

If you would like to order further copies of this book, or any of our other titles, then please give us a call or order via your online account.

Young Writers
Remus House
Coltsfoot Drive
Peterborough
PE2 9BF
(01733) 890066
info@youngwriters.co.uk

**Join in the conversation!
Tips, news, giveaways and much more!**

YoungWritersUK   YoungWritersCW
youngwriterscw   youngwriterscw